Praise for *Transitioning the Church*

Transition involves a change from one condition to another. The process of transitioning a church is often-times costly... If the church you serve is in the process of transitioning, I encourage you to allow Zach Williams to walk alongside you on this journey.

Dr. Steve Mullen
Dean, Mary C. Crowley College of Christian Faith, Dallas Baptist University

This book will challenge, inspire, and serve as a catalyst of change for the way in which the typical pastor views his role as a Christian leader. Any person seeking to cultivate the kind of congregation in passionate pursuit of Christ will discover practical and thought provoking truths that are sure to enlighten our thinking of how church ought to be.

Adam C. Wright
Vice President and Dean, Dallas Baptist University

In this book, Zach Williams proposes that these churches must transition focus away from themselves and onto the *unchurched,* keeping true to Christ's unchangeable *message* but tailoring their *methods* to effectively engage the lost in their culture.

Scott Sanford
Executive Pastor of Cottonwood Creek Baptist Church, Allen, TX, Texas State Representative

When it comes to your role in reaching the world, this book will make you uneasy with where you are and give you clarity on where you should be.

Jordan Easley
Pastor & Author of *Life Change*

Read it, and get God's heart for the unchurched!

Greg Surratt
Senior Pastor Seacoast Church
Author of *Ir-Rev-Rend*

Transitioning the Church offers a bold, fresh look at how or if your church is actually reaching your community. Zach offers great insight into how you can transition the culture of your church to focus on those who Christ lived and died for... the lost and hurting of your community that live outside of your church walls.

Marc Cleary
Director of Development - Association of Related Churches (ARC)

Acknowledgements

To my Jesus - thank you! No other words are needed.

To my wife - Ashley: you have been a huge encouragement to me. Thank you for all you do and put up with. You are a phenomenal wife, mother, and pastor's wife. I love you!

To my kids - Ava, Jack, and Pierce: as I pray over you each night, "God, thank you for creating these three kids to do incredible works for Your glory and kingdom and for the lives they will change." I love you!

To mom and dad - thank you for the example you have set for me and teaching me how to grow in faith, trust God, and stay faithful.

To Rainer Publishing - even though this was a dream, I never imagined it coming true. Thank you for the trust and opportunity.

To First Anna - thank you for allowing me to serve as your pastor. Let us continue to transition and reach those that are hurting, lost, and desperate.

Transitioning the Church

Leading the Established Church to Reach the Unchurched

Zach Williams

Published by Rainer Publishing

Contents

Introduction   1

Chapter 1   Transitioning   6

Chapter 2   Surrender   15

Chapter 3   Evaluating Ministries   23

Chapter 4   The Right Staff   31

Chapter 5   Is Your Church Ready?   43

Chapter 6   God's Desire for a
              Transitioning Church   57

Chapter 7   The Battle   65

Afterword   70

Introduction

Is the church primarily for the churched or the unchurched? However you answer that question, I hope you can agree the church should benefit people in both groups. This book is about a problem in many established churches: They have lost their drive to reach the unchurched. Unfortunately, this problem perpetuates because of church leadership. Too many church leaders are content with an inward focus. The mission of God is not designed to reach the churched. God seeks and saves the lost.

This is not true of all churches, pastors, and leaders as there are many healthy churches across our landscape that are spreading the message of Jesus and watching the Spirit work in their lives. These churches have decided to be proactive about their community rather than letting a few decades pass and then wondering, "Well, what do we do now?"

The focus of this book is on churches that have crossed the half-century mark. That is certainly not to say "newer" churches could not use this work as a guide, but older, established churches have a different way of thinking, one that has been ingrained in them and the people.

I have served in three churches full-time and another part-time; and each of these churches were established churches, three of them were deeply rooted in tradition and the other realized the need and desired to transition from the churched to the unchurched.

For the three churches entrenched in tradition, two of them were minimally impacting their area, even with neighborhoods surrounding them on every side, the attendees were making a concerted effort of driving there, passing multiple churches. Another church that had community people attending was shrinking in size simply because the desire to do anything different from how it had been done since the church first started was viewed with a heavy amount of skepticism.

With those three churches as my experience, like many of you pastors, staff, and leaders reading this book, it becomes a jaded experience, does it not? When we first started ministry, it was not about attendance and budgets. We were entering an area where we knew the costs before signing up. Yet along the way, something happened. We became content. We stopped chasing the unchurched because we were in a groove and pursing the unchurched simply requires too much work and effort.

My fourth church is different. The previous two pastors paved the way by making some hard decisions. Some of those decisions included changing the style of worship and forming a group to re-write the church bylaws, which will be expounded upon later in the book. The transitioning started prior to my becoming the pastor, and I am thankful that I did not have to make some of those decisions. There are still tough decisions to be made—now and in the future—but these two former pastors started our church down this road of transitioning and it is the path we are still on today.

Since transitioning an established church is a real problem in real life in real time, I'm using my church—First Anna in Anna, Texas—as a way to illustrate the process. Obviously, every church is different. But all established churches do share some leadership themes. Rather than working through concepts in hypothetical situations, I believe my church will help you apply this process to your context and leadership situation.

Transitioning is a process we are all familiar with in our own lives. From babies to toddlers to children to teenagers to adults and then to senior adults. Along the way, many lessons are learned and even more forgotten. The process has become hidden in our life as we experience change, we think nothing of it, until it affects something in that makes us uncomfortable. After all, the desire of every person is to be older, until you hit some arbitrary age in which you feel too old. Then you want to be young again. As we transition with our lives, we achieve what we desire: the process of aging.

But there are a few items in our life that we prefer not to transition. For many of us, this includes our church. With the world changing around us, our communities are changing faster than we would have ever imagined or even liked. Thus, the local church becomes the place where we can find solace, time standing still. While I understand this thinking, it happens at the peril (eternal peril) of the community at large.

One of the saddest comments I have heard from a person in our church was they thought they were too old for church. This thinking is not the heart of this book nor is it the heart of my church. Transitioning is a biblical principal found in Philippians 1:6: *And I am certain that God, who began the good work within you, will continue his work until it is finally finished on the day when Christ Jesus returns.* From this verse, Christ expects us to continue to transition, to continue to change into the image of His Son, to stretch and to grow. And if we believe that it is true with our personal relationship, why would we think it does not apply to the church body as a whole? We are never going to have it all right or everything together. The day we do have that mindset—that we do not have to transition—is the day the doors will shut.

Transitioning is one of the most important characteristics a church can have as it benefits the entire community and allows each person that attends to have a part as it shapes lives and communities. It is the mission of Jesus, to take those hurting and lost and give them life.

While this book is geared towards those in church leadership, it is easily adapted to the life of any believer. Maybe you attend church and a small group, read Scripture a few times a week personally, and that is the extent of your spiritual journey. But you find yourself stuck. You have the understanding that when Jesus died, He did so for you to do more than attend church. If this is you, and you are frustrated, then I pray this book will be helpful.

Both churches (corporately) and believers (individually) should stop settling for less. There is more to church than the mundane routine. There is more to your life. Let's begin the journey of transitioning.

Chapter 1

Transitioning

Don't copy the behavior and customs of this world, but let God transform you into a new person by changing the way you think. Then you will learn to know God's will for you, which is good and pleasing and perfect.
Romans 12:2

My church has a lot going against it, at least on the surface. We're in a small town. And we're the "First Baptist" in our town. The entire high school doesn't show up when you serve pizza anymore. The worship center doesn't fill to capacity just because you're having a revival. Those days are long gone.

Now, instead of just having special events and expecting to draw crowds, churches, pastors, and leaders have to be strategic in reaching their communities. There is only so much money and time available. Rather than do a few events a year and call it "outreach," what if churches and the leaders became focused on transitioning year-round? What impact would that have? First Anna desires attendees to continue attending church, to move from unchurched to churched to a thriving relationship with Jesus.

The definition of transition is to move from one place to another, and it's how we as church leaders should shape the churches in which we serve. Churches should be places of transition. What does that require? To move from unchurched to churches is a huge shift. To go from one to the other requires much on their part and ours. But it's also just the beginning. Churches, pastors, and leaders have to be strategic in reaching their communities.

Ask any pastor about whom the church should reach most. The obvious answer is the lost. But something happens as the pastor becomes entrenched in an established church. Over time, the fire to reach more becomes less bright. Routines and traditions are established, often unintentional, but they are still created. Church members begin to jockey for power and important positions. Frustration begins to surface. The focus is taken off the lost and those in the surrounding community and put onto the church itself. The mission that is supposed to be taking place outside the church has become entrenched within the four walls. It's a far too common story.

The process of becoming an established church happens slowly, and it is often an unintentional process. It just happens. At some point, many established churches stop doing what they were designed to do. They stop drawing people. They stop reaching outward. These churches can fall into the cycle of maintaining the existing state of affairs within the church. Maintaining rather than transitioning becomes the goal. Member needs and priorities become the focus. Is this what Jesus had in mind?

The shift towards maintenance does not start intentionally, but as priorities and goals shift, so does the mission. Church leader, if your goal is to reach the unchurched, are you doing it? Are you personally taking responsibility? Do you know a lost person? Honestly? A token response is not enough to prove it in the same way your desire to reach the unchurched is not enough. We can have plenty of plans and intentions of reaching the unchurched, but plans and intentions do not translate into action. Are you reaching the unchurched? Is your church transitioning along with the community of the church? Whether we like it or not, the community we serve is always in a state of transition. So our churches should also be in a constant state of transition.

Pastors and church leaders, I am one of the least qualified to write any kind of book or article to other pastors and church leaders. I never attended seminary. It was not my goal to be a pastor. I'm not exactly sure how it all happened. I just surrendered to the Holy Spirit, and something happened. As my ministry at First Anna began, I kept surrendering, and something took hold, first in me, then in the church leaders. And now it's making its way through our church. Power. But not man-made power. The Spirit's power is flowing through our church and in doing so, we are seeing something rare.

My encouragement to you, pastor and church leader, is if it can happen to us, then it can happen to you. Don't allow frustration to build and cynicism to remain inside you. You can transition from a churched crowd to an unchurched crowd. First Anna is in a rural area outside of Dallas-Fort Worth. We've been here for 165 years.

When you think of "First" churches, you usually think money because decades ago these churches were filled to capacity with tithing members. First Anna is unique in that this is far from our reality. There is no endowment. Spending freezes occur regularly. However, power overcomes lack of money, the power of the Holy Spirit that is.

According to statistics, First Anna is an average sized church. We as pastors and church leaders read books and articles that are authored by biggest and most known leaders. We go to the big conferences. I love to hear stories of how God is using these churches, but it becomes a little disheartening.

We ask these questions:

"What does this mean to us?"

"How are we supposed to relate to what they are saying? Do they even remember the struggles we encounter daily?"

"Sure, these are good theories and principles, but actually applying this to our church, well, it is just not possible."

Another unique quality we have is even though First Anna was established long ago, we are a young church with the average age in the late-30s. About 25 percent of our attendees are new in the faith or brand new to church. We have many unbelievers who attend our church regularly. We're still discovering how an established church can be a place for the unchurched. It's not easy. I hope the following chapters will inspire you to believe any church can get out of the ruts and start reaching new people.

This book will show you the steps we have incorporated to transition from the churched to the unchurched. Here's a warning. For some of you and the churches you lead, these steps will be controversial. You will cause discomfort among the churched in the congregation. Some will begin to eye you and the other staff and leaders with distrust because this is "their church." It is hard both emotionally and spiritually. As the pastor or church leader, you will question every decision you make as the backlash grows.

Is it worth it? This one question will arise in your head each and every day as you transition. The answer depends on how willing you are to fight for the transition. Is it worth it? If goal is to reach the lost and that is the goal you want to accomplish, then yes, it's worth it.

The church will lose some members during the transition. Many times those who choose to disengage from the church will be people that have been believers for a long time, maybe even a part of the inner-workings of the church. How does this affect the church? Finances will be impacted, and this is a hurt that ripples throughout the church. When a group of the establishment leave and take their tithe with them, new believers will often not fill in the financial gaps quickly.

Another effect of transitioning from the church to the unchurched is one that hurts pastors and leaders more than anything else: the gossip. I have been called a false teacher, a charismatic (a label that actually doesn't bother me), a bad pastor, and a weak pastor. These labels are just the ones I am aware of. In one meeting, someone actually looked me in the face and said they did not like me or the job I was doing, nor did they agree with the direction the church was going and how could God be happy with it. At least this person confronted me personally. Get ready. The criticism will come.

People will also say odd things about your church. First Anna has been called a Jewish cult (this one makes me laugh). I talk a lot about the Old Testament and often preach from the perspective of the Jews since that was the audience Jesus addressed. And we use matzah bread when we take communion.

We are criticized for the worship music, the sermons, the ministries, the people on the worship team (gasp...We have a divorced person who sings!). We've even allowed a non-Baptist to preach in our church.

Among the gossips, do you know what the common denominator is? If you have been in ministry long, the answer will not surprise you. The theme among gossips is they tend to be in the church. This realization shook me when I first discovered most churches have a group of people who can be quite mean. I felt like my ideals of ministry were less attainable when I had this realization.

The saddest and most frustrating part of the criticism is that it is rooted in fear. Once fear is entrenched in the lives of people, it is like an infestation that is extremely difficult to remove. What are some of these fears that the churched people have? They have a fear of losing the past (often called the "good old days"). They have a fear of losing stability. With the community changing, the church becomes the one stable point. New people threaten this cherished stability. They have a fear of the unknown. What will the unchurched do to our church if they start coming? "What happens if we continue doing this?" was a frequently asked question last year when more unchurched people started attending First Anna. My answer: "What would happen? More salvations, outreach, healings, and freedom. What's not to like?" Because we like to be in control in all aspects of our lives, the unknown offers no such control. And we love to control our churches.

The criticism First Anna encounters is not from the unchurched, but the churched. The unchurched, when they attend First Anna and discover our heart and see our desire to help "the least of these," are attracted to who we are. They see we are a different church that does not care about what happened in the pasts of people. We all have failures in our past and present life, but our God we worship desires to restore us where we leave condemnation behind and walk with Him. This is the message people need to hear yet it makes people uncomfortable, specifically the churched.

Are you ready for this? Are you ready to embark on the transitioning process? Are you ready for the criticisms? The friends leaving the church? The gossip? The frustrations and tears? Are you ready to be questioned at every decision made? Are you ready for new believers to enter the church and find salvation, healing, and freedom? Are you ready for the lost sheep? Is your church ready for the prodigal son to come home? If you are ready for this, the road is difficult but yes, it is worth it.

Chapter 2

Surrender

*Then he said to me, "This is what the LORD says to
Zerubbabel: 'It is not by force nor by strength, but by
my Spirit,' says the LORD of Heaven's Armies."*
Zechariah 4:6

"On the day of Pentecost, when the scoffers, and
the scorners said "These men are full of new
wine," Peter stood and exalted Jesus of Nazareth
and reminded Israel "that God hath made that
same Jesus, whom ye crucified, both Lord and
Christ." When Christ is truly honored, the Spirit
comes!"
- A.W. Tozer, *Day By Day*

The path you are about to embark on will require
much more than you currently have. Relying on
your power, strength, and intellect is not nearly
enough to accomplish the task of transitioning. On
our own, we are limited in all aspects. Even the
most intelligent pastor and leader is limited, and
the task we are faced with demands more than we
can humanly handle. During the transition, it is a
great comfort to realize that while we are limited,
the One that is unlimited wants to deposit His

power into us so we are not toiling and living in our own power, but in His.

Surrender. There will be times that you will want to surrender your position, your books and desk, just to get away because the road you are on is tiring, difficult, and at times heartbreaking. But the surrender needed to get on the path of transition is not to the deacon or elder board or the denominational headquarters or the wealthiest church member, it is a surrender to the Holy Spirit. While surrendering to the Spirit will not make the transition easier just as becoming a believer does not make one's life any easier, the Spirit gives us the strength and grace needed to get the church on the track God desires.

While I realize numerous theological differences exist about the indwelling of the Spirit, you have to admit when you read the New Testament, there are stark differences in the disciples, specifically Peter, after they are filled with the Holy Spirit. In the same way, the early church is starkly contrasted to the church of today, and the difference is more than lights and technology. The early church understood surrender. The disciples knew the mission they were on, which is the same mission you are on. It can only be accomplished through surrender.

Through surrender, the disciples transitioned from weak and scared humans to bold and courageous church leaders. How else can the transformation of Peter be explained? One minute he is lying and fussing to a teenage girl about his association with Jesus and a little later, he is standing before the religious leaders preaching to them about Jesus. Peter experienced his own transition.

Surrender is the most important step to transitioning the church or ministry you are leading. Jesus said that it is better for Him to go so the Holy Spirit could be sent. If the Holy Spirit is better to have here on earth, have you surrendered to the Spirit? Is He leading you and guiding you not only in your work as a pastor or church leader but also personally? Before you answer, how do you know? What is the evidence that you have surrendered to the Spirit?

If you have been at the church for any amount of time, and it is filled with only church people, this question should strike you: Are you following the Spirit? Does the Spirit only want churched people coming to church, or does He desire the lost and hurting? I'm afraid that often, we try to lead the Spirit into where we want to go rather than have Him lead us where He wants us to go.

While this step is the most important in seeking the transitioning of the church, it is often the most controversial because it refers to the part of the Trinity many Protestants (especially Baptists) talk about the least. I grew up Baptist and the only time I heard the term the Holy Spirit was when a person was baptized: "I baptize you in the name of the Father, of the Son, and of the Holy Spirit." I literally had no clue the role of the Holy Spirit. There is a difference in having head knowledge about the Holy Spirit and being surrendered to the Holy Spirit.

My mentor, Greg Surratt of Seacoast Church in Charleston, was passing through town when I sent a Twitter message to see if he wanted lunch. This day was my official first day as the pastor of First Anna. While we ate, I talked with him for over an hour and a half. In this conversation, Pastor Greg gave me a piece of advice that has stuck with me: "Have thick skin and a soft heart, and never mix the two up."

No truer phrase has been spoken to me, and I needed it earlier this year when friends of ours left First Anna. The reasons that were given varied. We weren't Baptist enough. We were too charismatic. We talked about the Holy Spirit too much.

These were all true statements. We did talk about the Holy Spirit often and for one reason: Jesus said it was better for Him to go so the Holy Spirit could come (John 16:7). If Jesus thought the Holy Spirit would be better for the disciples and us, then of course we should talk about Him.
What happens if we refuse to surrender to the Spirit's leading? We'll try to achieve success on our own terms. This power is limited. But the Holy Spirit's power is unlimited.

Another danger of surrendering to the Holy Spirit is that you and your ministry will be challenged. Your sermons, vision, and mission completely changes when you surrender. Before the church can transition from churched to unchurched, you as the pastor or leader must transition and become a Spirit-led leader. Only then can you lead a church to surrender—corporately—to the Holy Spirit.

The church will take its cue from you, as you have already discovered. As you talk about the Holy Spirit and what He is doing in your life, and you encourage them to read Scripture pertaining to the Spirit, He will become more accepted and as you talk about the Spirit leading you.

As both church and pastor surrender together to the Holy Spirit, both will embark on the same journey. I know because this corporate surrender is what First Anna has experienced. My first few sermons were over the Holy Spirit. Now, for a 32 year-old pastor preaching at a small-town First Baptist Church about the Holy Spirit and surrendering to Him, Vegas would have easily taken bets on how long my tenure at the church would last, with the over/under at three months.

Those first few sermons caused eyebrows to be raised and questions to be asked, but because of my walk with the Holy Spirit and the more I was learning about Him, no matter how difficult it became, I continued. At times when I was particularly discouraged, I began to experience the grace of the Holy Spirit in my life. He was providing me courage and encouragement. Each day I would get a text message, email, or phone call from someone offering encouragement. Now, as I write this, I reflect to that time and ask myself, how could I have gotten through that time had I not been on a discovery of the Holy Spirit?

Slowly it happened. Members of First Anna began to ask me and my wife questions. What are you reading? Why are we different from others in the church? As we answered and encouraged them to read Scripture, a change happened. What once was talked about hardly at all (except for baptisms: "I baptize you in the name of the Father, the Son, and the Holy Spirit.") was being studied and talked about openly.

Spiritual growth was happening in our church because as we embraced the Holy Spirit, and we began to know Jesus more. After all, the Holy Spirit pushes us to know Jesus. As spiritual growth happened and our church was maturing, we then started to move to a church for the unchurched.

First Anna is not a seeker-sensitive church. Neither are we a church that uses churchy jargon. Rather, we are a church that desires to honor God while reaching out to those that appear to have everything together, as well as those who have broken lives. The progression in this direction moved slower than I would have liked, but the slowness was necessary, so those that were on the fence as to what we were doing would understand the necessity of being Spirit-led to reach the unchurched. In other words, the people of the church saw that we were to reach the unchurched because they surrendered to the Spirit. He put that on their hearts.

Had we not focused on the Holy Spirit those first few weeks and then a few months later, I'm not saying First Anna would not have reached the unchurched, but it would have taken longer. The transition to focusing on the unchurched would have been more of a grinding change than the one we experienced. I would have become accustomed to the traditions and desires of the members. Instead, I was relying on the Spirit's power, and the church came along.

If you desire for the church to be the vessel that is used by God to reach the lost, bring hope to the hurting, comfort the brokenhearted, then it will require you stepping out of your comfort zone. Every church is different. Every context is different. Transitioning the church where God has placed you will require total surrender to the Spirit.

Upon this surrender, you will have the same grace and strength Jesus found in the Garden of Gethsemane. If Jesus found enough grace and strength to go to the cross, it will be enough to help you transition the church and reach those who are destined to be separated from God.

Surrender is the first step and most important step in transitioning the church because you 1) realize you need His power and 2) you realize it's not about you. The Holy Spirit used all sorts of people to spread the gospel. Stephen, James, and Peter are the first to come to mind, so realize the company you are in. The same Spirit that guided them to start the early church is guiding you to transition the church today!

Pastor, the Holy Spirit is concerned about each person, but do you think He is a little more aware of the lost? After all, believers are saved and ready for heaven, but the unbelievers?

Do you want to see the blessings of God? Then reach the lost. The reason Jesus left heaven was to reach the lost, and it should be our mission. To do so requires surrender to the Holy Spirit. Now what about the ministries of your church? The ongoing programming within the congregation is where people are put to work. Do these programs and activities have a focus on the lost? Not only do individuals need to surrender to the Holy Spirit in order to reach the lost. Not only does the corporate body need to surrender to reach the lost. We also need our programs and activities to have an outward focus. We'll examine this topic in our next chapter.

Chapter 3

Evaluating Ministries

Therefore, go and make disciples of all the nations,
baptizing them in the name of the Father and the
Son and the Holy Spirit.
Matthew 28:19

"Or suppose a woman has ten silver coins and loses
one. Won't she light a lamp and sweep the entire
house and search carefully until she finds it? And
when she finds it, she will call in her friends and
neighbors and say, 'Rejoice with me because I have
found my lost coin.' In the same way, there is joy in
the presence of God's angels when even one sinner
repents."
Luke 15:8-10

You've surrendered to the Spirit, now you're ready to transition, right? Walking in the power of the Holy Spirit is a necessary first step, but it's the beginning of this journey, not the end. In order to reach the lost and impact your community, you must evaluate the ministries the church offers.

As a disclaimer, not every ministry or program needs to be scrapped or retooled. Some are used for disciple-making, and some are used to draw in the unchurched. Evaluation is critical so that each program has a purpose and each ministry leader understands that purpose. Every ministry area should have this dual purpose, both to draw in those not connected to the church and to disciple those already within the church. Established churches, by their nature, have existing programs and ministries. Many times these ministries are entrenched in the culture of the church. This rootedness can good if there is a clear purpose to the program. Unfortunately, how many times have you sat at your desk and thought, "Why are we doing this?" Without a clear purpose, ministries in the church simply raise questions without answers.

One of the ministries I evaluated at First Anna was not an outreach or discipleship ministry. It was a tradition that was a huge drain on our budget. Every year, the church would have a breakfast for all graduating high school seniors. It's a small town tradition, and ours was no exception. Over 10 percnt of the student ministry budget and countless hours were poured into this one event that lasted approximately one hour. I am not even sure it was a service to the seniors. I think most of them came because their parents wanted them to come. There was absolutely no purpose behind this event other than it was done every year. On the surface, it was an easy decision to cancel the event. There were other places the money could go other than a breakfast. This event was evaluated, and we determined it met none of the purposes we are about: reaching the unchurched, discipleship, and service. We felt there was no point in continuing to do this event.

Was it hard? Not for me or the student pastor, but we had no emotional attachment to the event. For others in the church, they did not understand why we would do this. After going through the reasons for this decision, they still did not understand or agree. Emotional attachment and history are big hurdles that need to be overcome to transition from the churched to the unchurched.

We lost a few people when we started relying on the Holy Spirit, but the real trouble began when we started pulling up the sacred roots of long-standing ministries and programs. It's understandable. Some programs produced fruit for a season but are not outdated. Some people started certain ministries, and they have difficulty admitted what they created years ago no longer works. No committed person wants to see something they are involved in taken away.

If you think the criticism and gossip are bad, wait until you implement ministry and program changes. Finances and attendance will be impacted even more. Gossip will increase with statements like, "You don't care about our values or what we used to do." One of the reasons you must surrender to the Holy Spirit is because in times of transition you need God's grace to make it through the process of making difficult decision and implementing unpopular changes.

Each year I gather the staff of First Anna, and we evaluate the ministries we offer. As an established church, tweaking (we never "change" anything) and/or programming is one of the most difficult things to do. The ability to shift ministries and programs, however, is essential in the transitioning process and for the overall health of the church.

What happens if ministries are not tweaked? They become a type of ministry we never want to have: a "just because" ministry or program. A "just because" ministry serves no purpose other than existing. Why do we do this ministry? Just because. What is the purpose of investing in this program? Just because. Why do we allocate so much money to this area? Just because. The amount of time, money, and energy that staff and lay leaders put forth into a "just because" ministry offers no tangible results. Often these types of ministries offer no more than a congratulatory pat on the back where the churched look upon each other and say, "Great job!"

What are some "just because" ministries your church offers? What are the sacred cows that have been in the pasture a little too long? Where is the black hole of money and time that churns your stomach anytime someone mentions that ministry or program? If something isn't working, it something doesn't fit the vision of the church, then it needs to be cut so the money and energy can be put into other or new ministries that are capable of reaching the unchurched. The goal of the church is not maintaining ministries. The goal is reaching and discipling.

In an established church, entrenched ministries can drain the budget. For example, I cancelled one annual event that cost over 50 percent of the entire budget of that ministry area. The event had been going for 11 years, but it had run its course. It had been successful the first several years, but simply lost its effectiveness and was limping along. I re-directed that money to another part of the ministry that became one of the cornerstones of our church. At some point, the event I created will probably run its course, and the next pastor or church leader will need to eliminate it.

That is just one example. You can imagine what needs to be done throughout the church.

Eliminating ministries and programs doesn't need to be done just to do it so you can say, "Look at us. We are not afraid of change." Too many churches have only churched people attending because their ministries or programs are designed for them, not those on the outside. Evaluating ministries and programs requires more than symbolic changes to transition a church.

Maybe a ministry does not need tweaking. Maybe your heart needs to change concerning a ministry or program. Maybe you need the tweaking. If there is a ministry you do not prefer, but it is reaching the unchurched, then why eliminate it? Can you not grow to love it? Your preferences should not weigh on the decision to eliminate or start ministries. Be careful that you are not tweaking and eliminating programs and ministries simply because you do not like them. Before doing so, ensure they are not reaching the unchurched or discipling others. Why tweak a ministry that is accomplishing its objective?

How can you know? How can we ensure we have the ministries that align with our vision of reaching the unchurched? It takes evaluate lot of time to evaluate correctly. Meet with individual staff members to review their ministries. Make sure they are aware it is not a reflection on them or their service, but rather to see which ministries need to be tweaked or eliminated. This evaluation should be done annually with consideration of the demographic changes in the community. In fact, far too few churches evaluate ministries while also considering the changing demographics of their communities.

As you meet with the staff members and lay leaders, write down the purpose for the ministry being evaluated and have the staff member or leader explain how that particular ministry correlates to the church vision. Often, we forget the purpose of a ministry or event as we discuss the operational details of making it happen. This lack of focus means we probably have no clue if we are doing a "just because" program or not. Some ministries will be for the churched (discipleship) and some for the unchurched (outreach). But if a ministry currently exists for the sake of tradition, then celebrate its history and put it in the past. It will not be easy to do, but the results of the purpose will be undeniable.

As you evaluate the ministry down to the last detail, keep notes as to why the decision to eliminate it was made. In this way, those who disagree with the decision can understand. For the churched to fully comprehend this new direction, the vision of each ministry and program must be clear. Without this clarity, the ministries and programs of the church will exist in silos. Without this clarity, each ministry area will not move in the same direction.

The final decision to make in these meetings is whether to announce the ministry or program elimination or ignore it. As our church transitioned from the churched to the unchurched, I did both. Sometimes I announced the end of a ministry. Sometimes I simply ignored the ministry and let it die naturally. Ignoring the death means less immediate pain, but it often comes at the expense of later clarity. Announcing the death feels like ripping off a Band-Aid, but people clearly understand what is happening. Ultimately, you must address your congregation. And some people will be unhappy no matter how you handle it.

One of the ministries I am constantly evaluating is our Sunday School ministry. For those in newer churches or plants, you are thinking, "Why have Sunday School? Just go with groups." For those in established churches, the type of churches that need to transition, you are saying, "Why do you need to evaluate Sunday School? I mean, it's Sunday School!"

Currently we have two small groups - morning and evening. It may seem like overkill but both of them are reaching a different group of people so a purpose is being served. But, and this is a tough question for us, what if Sunday School stops reaching its purpose? As First Anna continues to transition from churched to unchurched, that will be one of the questions that arises in ministry evaluations.

Some changes require communicating to the entire church. Other changes require communicating only to the ministry area involved. As a church leader, however, you must address the dedicated people affected by the change. They must know your reasoning. Opposition will come. But you can guarantee opposition by not informing people affected by changes.

Chapter 4

The Right Staff

Work brings profit, but mere talk leads to poverty!
Proverbs 14:23

*And I have been a constant example of how you can
help those in need by working hard. You should
remember the words of the Lord Jesus: 'It is more
blessed to give than to receive.'"*
Acts 20:35

The staff you hire will speak volumes as to the
type of person you want to reach: the churched or
unchurched. The hiring assumes you have the
authority to do so, something that will be
addressed in a further chapter detailing how to set
the church up from a legal standpoint as it
transitions from churched to unchurched.

What happens if a staff person is hired by you or is
already serving at the church when you accept the
pastorate, and you realize they do not like
transitioning? If you are a staff member or
ministry leader, what do you do if you are faced
with an adult that has served in your ministry area
for years or decades?

Other than a growing relationship with Jesus and walking in the Spirit, having the right people in place is the most important decision you will make as a pastor or ministry leader. The staff and ministry leaders are an extension of you. You do not need staff. You need the right staff. If you are a ministry leader, then the same applies. You need people to come along beside you to minister with the same vision and goal.

Putting the right people in the right places can expedite the transitioning process. Putting the wrong people in the right places creates unnecessary hurdles in the transitioning process. And putting the wrong people in the wrong places just makes everyone miserable. Three key questions can help church leaders get the right people in the right ministry areas.

1. Are they on board with the vision?

Each leader should be on board with the vision of the church. It is a given, or at least you would think. Shortly after arriving at my church, I realized that I was not on the same page as some of the staff. The vision was not even there, and it appeared we were going through the motions. Going through the motions is tolerable but never enjoyable. They joy of the church comes from transformation, and transformation requires transitioning.

The ministry and church takes its cue from the leader or pastor. To create safeguards to ensure the ministry is fulfilling the vision of the church, the leaders must be doing so in their personal lives. The pastor must be personally living out the vision of the church so the people see the importance and need of it. If the pastor is not on board with the vision, it will show in his personal and ministerial life, and no one else will be either.

The mission of Jesus is found in Luke 19:10. He came to seek and save the lost. If that is what Jesus was passionate about, if that is what consumed Him, should we not follow? Should the passion of Jesus not be our passion as well? Does the vision and mission of the church reflect Jesus' mission to see people saved? Are the staff members or ministry leaders living the vision of the church?

Is God more concerned about church attendance or salvations? Scripture memory or salvations? Giving or salvations? Serving or salvations? Attendance, memorization, giving, serving, and other actions of a believer are important, but too often those traits become duties. When this sense of duty occurs, people lose the joy of why they worship. When a church loses sight of the mission, transitioning stops, and the focus becomes maintaining.

What happens if a staff member is not on board with the vision of the church, if they are not living it in their daily lives? I am telling you right now, without question, the relationship will not work. What will happen is the church will be fractured from within. When the staff has competing visions, the church will be pushed in different directions. Competing visions always mean competing goals. Unity with the vision is a must or the church will not transition and will fall into stagnation.

Have you seen stagnant water before? The water level drops in a river or lake, and the water becomes trapped with no movement. The water in the low levels becomes infested with all sorts of nastiness and is of no use to anyone. That is what a church looks like where the staff is not unified with their vision.

The senior pastor is the one person with the predominant task of developing the vision of the church, while the staff and leadership have to decide if they can submit to the authority of the pastor. With everyone working together, the incredible can happen. If the staff and leaders are split, going their separate ways, stagnation occurs.

2. Are the staff or leaders committed to reaching the unchurched?

Most churches will answer affirmatively to the question of reaching the unchurched. But what does their programming say? Some say "yes," but their programming says otherwise, and that is the reason for yearly evaluations. If at some point you do not see the staff member committed to the process of transitioning, this will sound harsh or even mean, but you should let them go. The goal is not to maintain a large ministry. The goal is to share the gospel with as many people as possible.

To ensure a smoother transition (rarely is anything truly smooth) during the process of adjusting the goals of the church, each staff member and ministry leader must be on board with transitioning from churched to unchurched. This focus must be their commitment above anything else. When it is, they have the same heart as Jesus had, who left His throne in heaven for those that were lost.

Here is how the cycle works. The staff takes their cue from the pastor. The ministry leaders take their cues from the staff. If the staff fails to catch your vision of transitioning or reaching the unchurched, the ministry leaders will have no clue what to do or why it is important. If the ministry leaders are confused as to what to do, then you will get confusing results from your church ministries.

If transitioning is important to you as the pastor, meet regularly with the staff and have conversations with them regarding their ministries. Ask them how they are equipping people to reach the unchurched and engage with them. Hear directly from them; do not guess as to what you think they are doing. Let the staff see how vital transitioning is to the life of the church and mission of Jesus.

What happens if staff and leaders are not committed? Face it, not everyone, even those who are paid to be there, will like transitioning. When transitions start, everything changes. Staff and leaders may feel as if the church is worrying only about growing numerically or the church is only concerned with new people. Some will feel the faithful have been forgotten.

The staff and leaders are not the only ones that will have this mindset, but if you can ease their minds and see they are committed to the vision and importance of transitioning, then they will be the ones who will be able to extinguish many of the fires that are started. So, what do you do if the staff and leaders within the church are not committed?

When you notice that one of the staff members is not "getting it," meet with that person. If you are a staff member and notice the same behavior from one of the ministry leaders—do the same—meet with him or her. In this meeting, seek out what is at the core of their reasoning for not wanting to transition. Often, staff members and pastors create their own traditions without realizing it.

Maybe one of the reasons they are not on board is the realization of something they created is no longer going to be essential or part of the ministry anymore. It's reasonable that people want to hang on to things. You must take the time to explain why transitioning is important. If you believe in transitioning, then it's worth your time to talk to people about why it is important.

There can be disagreements between the pastor and staff, but when it comes to the vision—the transitions—everyone has to be on board. This does not mean the staff and leaders become "yes" people, but it does mean they must have general agreement on the transitioning effort. The pastor, staff, and ministry leaders must be on the same page when it comes to vision and transitioning, otherwise you fight against yourself. One group will transition, while another group will not. A split in the vision is simply not going to be effective.

At a conference I attended, one of the keynote speakers said if a church tries to reach everybody, they will reach nobody. In two years, we have discovered at First Anna who we are as a church and whom we are trying to reach.

What we first decided was that we would not be a church for everybody. Our church is different, and not everyone that walks in is going to like it. We're fine with that. Understanding that we could not be the church for each person in our community, I led them to understand the reason Jesus came to earth, which was for the lost and how, as I have written multiple times through this book, if that was the mission of Jesus, then why are we not doing the same?

At a senior adult Bible study I lead once a month, I proposed a question to them that was similar to the preceding paragraph. We understand that God does not love some more than others. He has no favorites, but and this is the question: Where does God want the efforts of the church placed? Does God care a little more for those that are lost, that they might be found? This led to a great discussion. This group of senior adults, churched people, was able to see my heart on this subject.

One of the couples attending the Bible study has children older than I, and they spoke to the question from their perspectives as parents. They always enjoy hearing from their children with whom they have a good, strong relationship. However, when the "distant" child calls, there is a different kind of joy and excitement they experience.

God loves us all, but does He get a little more excited when He sees lost people begin to pursue Him? That is what we are about at First Anna, and we make no apologies for it. If you are churched, a believer, awesome, then you have eternal life and hopefully are living an abundant life on earth. Now, your job is to share that hope and restoration you received with others. We expect our members and attendees that have a relationship with Jesus to be committed to the cycle of transitioning.

One last thought before we move on: I am of the mindset that if only churched people are attending a church, it is probably time to close the doors. Controversial yes, but what good is the church doing? They have lost the fire and desire. Their commitment to reach the unchurched has vanished. The churched people may have community, which is a necessity for all believers, but the lack of transitioning causes them to forsake the Great Commission. A good staff leads a church to stay focused. And without this focus, the church loses its sense of purpose.

3. Why are they on staff?

Pastors and church staff often fall into one of two categories: they are lazy or they are hard workers. Ministry attracts those who like to cruise. Ministry attracts those who put the pedal to the metal.

We all know lazy staff members. They enjoy the paycheck. They like the conditions in which they work. The job is not physically demanding. They are able to make their own schedule. And the list goes on. By the same token, we all have seen demanding, work-a-holic pastors and staff as well. They don't know when to stop, when to close the computer, or put away the cell phone.
I knew one student pastor who went to a movie weekly while he was supposed to be working. It was not part of a group or anything. He went there by himself. Another played two rounds of golf every week. With tendencies like a poor work

ethic, the effort that is necessary to reach the unchurched simply will not be put forth. When staff are more concerned with getting out of work than actually working, transitioning is not an option due to the labor required.

I hired a student pastor a month prior to Easter. It was my second hire, and I was feeling great concerning the decision. During the multiple interviews, I informed him we would be having a Saturday night service for the crowds expected on Easter weekend. The week after coming aboard as our student pastor, he asked if it was necessary for him to be at the Saturday service. I knew then I had made a mistake in hiring. Throughout his short tenure at First Anna (he left four months later), he had a desire to reach the unchurched. His heart was in the right place, but he did not have a strong enough work ethic to follow through on his plans. Transitioning requires work, a lot of work, a lot of discipline, and without it, transition will simply not happen.

During the interview process and in their evaluations, ask your staff and ministry leaders, "Why are you here?" Let them tell you why they desire to continue serving at the church. Keep track of their responses through the years so you can see the path they are on.

These three questions are not a guaranteed way to ensure that the staff and ministry leaders will catch the vision to transition, but it is a start. Once the staff is on board, when you evaluate their ministries and programs, everyone is on the same page with the same understanding. When dealing with ministry leaders in key positions, include them in meetings and evaluations, even volunteers. First Anna has one full-time staff, five part-time staff, and three others that are laity but are treated like staff. I tell the three lay leaders "no" just like I tell everyone else. When the staff submits quarterly goals to me, they know they are expected to as well. I praise them as I do staff and give them direction as well. Even though they are laity, I treat them as paid staff because that is what they want. They want to play a role in transitioning, and without them it would be a lot harder.

As the pastor, you have a huge platform—literally the platform (or stage or pulpit, whatever you want call it). The staff, however, often has more direct influence. They are the ones interacting with the church in specific ministry areas. The pastor's role is to equip the staff and core leaders. The role of the staff and core leaders is to equip their areas. As a result, the often have greater numbers of close contacts. If the pastor tries to transition the church by himself, he will look like a dictator, and often, that is the result. Again, I speak from experience.

But when the pastor, staff, and leaders work together, the transitioning becomes both more effective and efficient. Everyone is made to feel a part of the team and feel, rightly so, their contributions are valued. With the wrong staff and leadership, transitioning will be more painful than it already is, if not impossible. But with the right staff and leadership, while still painful, it is a much more enjoyable experience.

Chapter 5

Is Your Church Ready?

Now I say to you that you are Peter (which means 'rock'), and upon this rock I will build my church, and all the powers of hell will not conquer it.
Matthew 16:18

You are surrendered to the Holy Spirit. Ministries are aligned with the vision—some of the programming tweaked. Staff and ministry leaders are on board. The unchurched are beginning to attend the church. And, as a result, a few people have left the church. You are realizing the vision. There is one problem. People are beginning to talk about who doesn't attend the church anymore. The one spot that had been occupied for many years no longer is, or worse, someone else is in the seat.

As you transition, you can expect the giving of the church to drop temporarily. If you publish your financials in an e-newsletter, bulletin, or income statement, then expect a group of people to question the changes when the giving goes down. We had a 20 percent dip for several months shortly after the transitioning started. I do not know who gives how much money in my church. But because the total giving dropped after certain people left, I assumed we lost some givers. I was told three of the top ten giving families had left First Anna. Our budget was not big to begin with, and losing that amount was tough.

Honestly, results like this make you as the pastor question the transition. I would often have conversations with myself, "If I stop this…" "If I don't push this as hard…" It would all end with, "…everything would be fine. Attendance and giving would go back to what it was." But I knew that was not the answer. Deep down I knew it, but it was a struggle not to revert back to how it was before transitioning started. Leaders will question how ministries are going to be paid for because people have stopped giving. Most likely, these financial issues are coming if you embark on transitioning.

Is your church ready for this? You need to prepare them for the transition. Let them know what the short-term future probably looks like once you start this path so they are not surprised and question even more than they will. Inspire them with a picture of the future in which more people are saved. Show them heaven will be a little more crowded and life on earth will be lived a little more abundantly because of a decision they made: To transition from an inward focus to an outward focus.

While the scope of this book does not allow for me to cover each area of the church comprehensively, let me walk through some major areas that will affect most churches in transition. The rest of this chapter will deal with these areas.

Bylaws

Aside from spiritually getting ready to transition, there is a legal document in many churches that needs to be reviewed to ensure that you as the pastor have both authority and accountability. Without authority, your leadership decisions could be derailed. Without accountability, you can derail yourself. The document is known as the church constitution or bylaws, and it is often viewed more sacred than Scripture in many denominational circles. It's enough to churn stomachs. But it's a necessary document in the life of the church.

When was the last time you read the constitution and bylaws? Is it set up for success or failure? Does the pastor have the ability to make changes, or must changes go before a board of some type? The bylaws should protect the pastor and church, not limit the leadership in the day-to-day operations and vision of the church. Sadly, they do more limited than protecting in most churches.

Many of these documents are written so certain people can have control and power. The pastor prior to me at First Anna took the task of creating a new church constitution. This new document gives the pastor both authority and accountability. Major decisions go to the elders, but other decisions are made by the pastor. Shortly after I started my pastorate at First Anna, a member came and asked if I was going to have more business meetings where the church could vote more. I explained that we are not that kind of church. Scripture was not enough for him, so then he asked, "Well, what do the bylaws say?" After a short conversation, he mumbled, "We need to change them." The bottom line was he no longer had the power to control the church.

This issue is a problem for the churched, not the unchurched. The unchurched are not thinking about power grabs in the congregation. They're not even there to know! Here is our answer to people who attempt power grabs: "If you want power, then you are at the wrong church. But if you want to change the community, then you are at the right church." Submitting to authority is a biblical principle, but it is not one we all like, especially when we disagree with the vision of the church or the decisions that those in authority are making. But God put the authority structure in place not only for our protection but also for our benefit.

The bylaws of the church should not hamstring the pastor. But the bylaws should allow him to make decisions as the Spirit leads. In many Baptist churches, deacons run everything. They are the decision makers. While many younger churches have a deacon body that is more Scriptural, many established churches still struggle with a controlling deacon board. Part of transitioning an established church is breaking the culture of allowing the church bylaws to trump Scripture.

I encourage you to read through your bylaws. As you read through them a second time, make notes of what should be changed. Remember to keep the keys of accountability and authority in mind. Both must be balanced to have a healthy set of bylaws. Pastors must have the authority to make decisions, but pastors must also be held accountable by some group or system in the church. Our church has a group of elders. I take major decisions to them for their guidance, while the day-to-day operations are left with the staff's discernment.

As you mark changes, pray over them. Are the changes you propose stemming from your human desires, or are they led by the Spirit? If from the Spirit, gather who the bylaws indicate are the "decision-makers," and share with them the promptings you are having in re-working the bylaws so that it aligns more clearly with Scripture.

The wrong set of bylaws will not only limit your ability as pastor, but also limit the church you serve in reaching its full potential. The right set of bylaws will give you the freedom to fulfill your vision to transition, and the wrong set will ensure the church is structured and organized in such way that the pastor and staff are nothing but puppets. And the unchurched are not drawn to puppet shows.

Worship Services

Take a Sunday off from preaching and just sit in the service and take notes. Even better, pay an unchurched person to come to church and write a report about the experience. Tell all the staff and key ministry leaders to do the same. Compare the reports. I'm sure the results will surprise you. Churches that make the transition look at their worship services through the eyes of the unchurched.

Prior to becoming pastor, I would take my family, and we would go to a Saturday evening service in the Dallas-Fort Worth area. It was not worship for me, but instead, I analyzed what was happening. I am timing the length of the announcements, the length of worshipping through music, the sermons, the décor, the phrases said by church staff and leaders. I took it all in. When I came to First Anna, it hit me. I needed to do the same thing for my church.

So one Sunday I did not preach. I sat in our worship service and observed. I wanted to view the worship services not through the eyes of the pastor, but through the eyes of someone that not had been to First Anna, or any church for that matter. I made notes of things to change or address throughout the service, but it was not enough. After all, no matter how fair I tried to be, I was biased. This was First Anna, and I was the pastor. What I thought needed to be changed (tweaked) could be different from what the unchurched might believe needs to be changed.

After this experiment, I called an old college roommate and asked both him and his fiancé to attend the following Sunday. I believe their observations would be helpful because 1) They had never been to First Anna and 2) No one knew who they were. Their job was simple: attend the worship service and take notes. I asked them to note the friendliness of our people, the ease of walking though the building, the first impressions of the space, the flow of the worship service, the music, and the sermon.

I wanted to know all of this information so that we could become better in reaching and meeting people and better at worshipping. Through this exercise I discovered we took a lot of stuff for granted. We made too many assumptions of guests. In short we had a lot of church jargon that we used. I realized many guests would probably not understand our "church-ese."

Try this same exercise at the church you serve. There are professional people that can help, but we were a church with financial struggles and could not afford to pay someone. So I used people I knew from a variety of age groups and they would anonymously come and "shop" the church.

As staff and leaders, we become oblivious to some of the things in our church. Especially with our worship services, we could use a fresh perspective. As you being the transitioning process in the church you serve, each week, you will discover people from the community that are eager to see what is happening. It's tough. But it's also exciting.

This process of evaluation has refined the goal of our worship services. Our goal of a worship service is not to give talented people a chance to perform. Rather, our goal is for those attending to discover God and lay their burdens aside. We want all people who attend our church to escape to the arms of Jesus where the hopeless find hope and encouragement. If worship does anything other than magnify Jesus, it is not worship. Our goal is to be Jesus-centered in everything. But as we glorify Christ, we explain to our attendees why we are worshiping. Don't miss this important point. You cannot assume guests will pick up on the church jargon. Even more importantly, you cannot assume they will grasp the why of worship.

When I was still the student pastor at First Anna, the elders asked me to step up until a pastor was found and during this time, I had the authority to do what was needed. The worship service order bothered me because we would sing a song or two and then have 10 minutes of announcements. I had seen other churches do announcements at the end of the church, but that took away from the experience and presence of God.

As we started to transition, I did not care if the unchurched heard the announcements, but I did care if they heard about the Jesus. So I moved announcements to the very beginning of service. This one little adjustment made an impact not only on those in attendance worshipping, but also our worship team. Our goal is not announcements, but to show people Jesus and how He can save and restore them.

At First Anna, we do not tailor our church services towards the churched or unchurched. The environment we create makes the unchurched feel welcome and encourages spiritual engagement for both parties. Our worship services are Gospel-centered and life applicable from the beginning to the end. Our desire is for the believers to worship and use the worship service as an opportunity to step into the presence of God corporately. For the unchurched, the desire we have is for them to see Christ and how Scripture relates to all aspects of life. In this way, we have to meet both the churched and the unchurched where they are.

As churches transition to the vision of Jesus, worship services have to as well.

Facilities

The facilities at First Anna are, well...where do I start? Two buildings are portable and are falling apart, but somehow, many years ago, that pastor decided it would a good idea to go into debt for them. Two other buildings are from the 1930s and have not been touched on the exterior since being built. And it shows. We have two parking lots, both of which are dirt because the gravel has washed away. When I came to the church as student pastor, one and a half years prior to becoming pastor, the worship center was condemned.

Needless to say, our facilities do not present an image of a church that is alive. But on the inside, now that's a different story. Exterior building work is very expensive. For churches that are transitioning, it is difficult to update facilities. But one thing that can be done cheaply is keeping the facilities clean. Cleanliness is a lot more important than the physical looks of the building. If I'm in the movie theater, then I like it to be clean. If I'm in a restaurant, then I expect a level of cleanliness. Guess what? The unchurched have the same expectations of a church should they decide to visit one Sunday.

Look at it this way: The unchurched are our target audience as we transition. People in America are consumers. Our mission field (target audience) are consumers. What do consumers want? What do they expect? Excellence. Cleanliness. They want to know they are valued. And we should devote time and energy to make them know they are valued.

The majority of those attending First Anna have either babies or children. What would a parent's thought be if when the drop off area of the children's ministry had not been cleaned? If filth was on the walls and dirt on the floor, then how would you expect them to react?

Facilities are costly, yet when it comes to transitioning our churches, it is well worth the expense. For those reading this that have problems with big buildings and the amenities that go along with them, remember our target: consumers. Part of being contextual in our culture is meeting expectations, at least in part, when it comes to facilities. We simply do not live in a part of the world where buildings are optional. The mission field is growing each and every day, and the churches need to contextualize their facilities in the communities in which they reside. It's an expensive but necessary part of transitioning.

Scheduling

Another area of the church to consider during the transitioning process is the scheduling of the pastor and staff members. I enjoy meeting with and learning from other pastors and staff members. I am never afraid to ask for help because even after eleven years in ministry, I still wonder what I am doing. The growth First Anna has experienced, I call it stupid growth. I call it that because we have no growth campaigns, mass mail outs, or anything else. We have a church, targeted ministries, and an expectation God will show up in incredible ways.

My desire is not to have the biggest church but to have the unchurched in our community attending and active in a Bible-teaching church. First Anna is not for everyone, and I tell guests that each week. I tell them if this church is not for you, then let us know and we will help you find a place to plug in. Those are not empty words either, but sincere. Each community needs several healthy churches because one church cannot do it all.

Because we have had stupid growth, I have been required to play catch-up in what to do. When I meet with pastors for advice, one of the first questions I ask is, "What am I supposed to be doing?" Without fail, throughout the conversations, I've been told by many of them to act twice the size you are as a church.

The first thoughts running through my head when receiving such advice is, "Why be something I am not?" I could picture the ego and pride coming into my life when I, with a church of 200 start acting bigger than what is needed. When First Anna approached 400, how could I possibly act and structure the church like we were 800? When we reach 800, why would we act like 1,600? As the conversations progressed I found out why to follow that paradigm. We structure that way now so when those numbers are reached, the church is not playing catch-up. The point is to arrive at the structure a little before the numbers get there.

When I transitioned from student pastor to lead pastor, we were around 200 attendees. We were running everything as the size we were until I started meeting with other churches, and they were showing me what they had learned the hard way. Adjustments were made, but it is still something we have to question often by asking, "When First Anna is 400, what will my schedule look like? What will my day-to-day be? What will others be doing?" We have those answers in place currently and this has allowed for an easier transition. The easier the staff can transition during this cycle, the easier the church can as well.

Since we aren't at 400 yet, we have not adjusted to act like First Anna is running 800 but we are planning on it. One of the items I am working on for myself is my schedule. My goal is to be accessible to as many people as possible, yet I also want to protect my time. I have found those within the church that are closest to me, protect my time more than I do. They realize I personally cannot meet the needs of each member. I have staff and leaders I have given authority to help in this area.

I was given insight in this area from one of the pastors I admire, Pastor Greg, and his assistant. While visiting Seacoast Church over the course of a few days, I saw that Pastor Greg was always talking to people after the services in the foyer. I asked how often he did that because at other churches of that size and even smaller, I have seen pastors that completely cut themselves off from the people and their church. I was shocked how one of the most influential men in church and the pastor of an incredibly large church could do so. I discovered he does that after each service, each week, until everyone that wants to talk with him is through.

There is a fine line to walk because if the pastor, staff, and ministry leaders are not cautious, pride kicks in, and it becomes about reaching that next level of growth or acting in a certain way. And those become goals rather than seeing the unchurched seeing the need for salvation and freedom.

Chapter 6

God's Desire for a Transitioning Church

"If a man has a hundred sheep and one of them gets lost, what will he do? Won't he leave the ninety-nine others in the wilderness and go to search for the one that is lost until he finds it? And when he has found it, he will joyfully carry it home on his shoulders. When he arrives, he will call together his friends and neighbors, saying, 'Rejoice with me because I have found my lost sheep.' In the same way, there is more joy in heaven over one lost sinner who repents and returns to God than over ninety-nine others who are righteous and haven't strayed away!"
Luke 15:4-7

Chris Hodges is the pastor at Church of the Highlands in Birmingham, Alabama. He has greatly impacted my life and ministry. We were having a conversation about the Holy Spirit once, and he told me one of Highlands' mottos. It was so good that I stole it and have used it several times, "We will do anything, short of sin, to see people saved." Powerful statement, right?

Why is this statement so important? Because Jesus lived it out. It was evident in His life until He said His last words on the cross. He hung with the sinners while others were quick to turn their backs on them and regard them as second-class citizens.

As you read New Testament Scripture, observe how Jesus and John the Baptist spoke both to and about the religious leaders. They were referred to as snakes, which is interesting since that is the how Satan appeared in the Garden of Eden to deceive Eve. Have you noticed the only time the gospels record Jesus upset was with the religious leaders? He was never agitated with sinners because His heart was for the sinners. His heart was to see transitions—from sinner to saved. God has a heart for those that are lost and desires for transitions.

Jesus healed, loved, comforted, and desired to see life changes. He did whatever it took to see it. Paul had the same desire in Romans 9:3. He was willing to be cut off from Christ to see his people saved. He was willing to do the unthinkable to see transitions.

For us, though, as churched people, if something in our life becomes even a little uncomfortable, then then we think twice before proceeding. If it goes against our traditions or attendance and giving drops, we have conversations as to whether or not we are doing the right thing. It is easy to proclaim, "This is the path we as a church will travel down regardless of who may come against us and how much we are criticized." After all, Romans 8:31

reminds us that if God is for us, then what else is there? It is easy to state, but once the journey starts and opposition does mount, it becomes completely different. Doubt and fear set in. You have to trust God's promises like never before.

God's desire is for the church to transition, for the unchurched to have a relationship with Him, for believers to grow more to be more like Jesus. He wants each person in a transition, never satisfied with their past or present spiritual successes, but in close relationship.

We know God's desire—that no one should perish—but realistically people will. Billions of people will die and be separated because they have no relationship with Jesus. Some because they never heard even though they have creation all around to testify to the majesty of a Creator. Some of them are in my small town. Some of them are in your town, neighborhood, or city.

Many churches are often too concerned with keeping out who does not belong, whether that is those who do not look like them, act like them, and have a past like them. I hesitate to say it, but I believe many established churches are like this.

Recently, there was a couple who visited one of our services. I was stopped by a member after the service they attended and said they were concerned because the couple, both men, had their arms around each other and wanted to know what

I was going to do about it. I simply said nothing, we welcome each person here. And if I was to start asking certain people to leave, should I say, "If you have looked at porn this week, you are no longer welcome here." What is the difference, I asked. After a few seconds of silence, this person said, "Good point." And really, where else would we rather them be? Is this not the place we want them, a place where they can encounter the love, restoration, and freedom that our Jesus offers.

Another time I was stopped by a well-intentioned church member between services. This member was upset that one of the attendees was wearing shorts and a hat in the service. This person was visibly upset at the lack of respect shown. I handed my iPad to them, which is what I preach from, and asked them to find a Scripture verse that says a person attending church has to wear slacks or a suit.

We churched people are far too guilty of being way too concerned that someone is going to look so different from us, it scares us. We are afraid of the people we claim we want to reach. When they begin attending church, we get in our groups and pretend they are not here and make comments about how they look or smell. We want them to look like us, when they should look nothing like us. I do not want those that are unchurched, as they transition, to look like the churched. I want them to look like Jesus.

This is why a vision is important. People get off track when the vision of the church is not prominent. These scenarios happens when there is no vision, no mission, and the church does "church things" just because that is what a church does.

Do the people attending the church know what your vision is? Are they aware of the seriousness of "doing church" while forsaking the lost? Many in American churches have been attending for so long, the fire within them has flamed out, and now everything they do is out of habit and routine.

I challenged First Anna with this very thing in a recent sermon. Think back to when you first became a believer. Remember that fire, the desire that was within you? For some, it has been two years, others fifty years. What happened to it? Where did it go? Now, instead of transitioning, we have grown content with our routine, our habit. We have lost our vision, our dream and all that we wanted to accomplish. We wanted to set the world on fire and now, we want to hide in our traditions and routines. We have no personal vision, so we live mundane religious lives.

What does a personal vision look like? It's simple. Read about the life of Jesus and imitate His life. Our personal and spiritual vision should not be tied to any one denomination but to Christ alone. This verse has become key to us at First Anna as we transition, and it serves as a reminder that it is solely about Jesus and nothing else. Colossians

3:11: "In this new life, it doesn't matter if you are a Jew or a Gentile, circumcised or uncircumcised, barbaric, uncivilized, slave, or free. Christ is all that matters, and he lives in all of us." Christ is *all* that matters. That is it. Nothing else, only Jesus.

Just like with all of the chapters so far, there is resistance when it comes to Jesus from the churched people. This is a controversial statement but if you are serving in an established church, ask the churched people how many unchurched people they are friends with or when the last time was they spent time with the unchurched.

First Anna has been called a church that is not "Baptist enough." One person that left our church said that while we are not doing anything that is not biblical, it's not Baptist enough. Another has asked, "What does the Southern Baptist Convention think of what we are doing?" Many of the churched people in our church were more focused on our denomination than Jesus. They could not see Jesus because of denominational affiliation.

What's more important to people in the church you pastor or lead, the denominations or Jesus? Believers, pastors, leaders, will you do anything to reach the lost, even if it means forgoing what people want or expect from a church? If you desire to see the church transition and reach the lost, then you will find it is well worth it, no matter the struggles you encounter on the path. Christ is all that matters.

Instead of transitioning, we often try to placate those that are in the church, those that are saved. We are often more concerned with those that are saved than those that are lost and have no relationship with Jesus. We have ministries, programs, and worship services designed for those that are already going to heaven. We cannot transition because we are stuck. Our focus has shifted. Christ is all that matters.

After I became the pastor, I was under the impression I needed to hurry and develop a vision for the church so people could see what we were about, and I would sit and think and write catchy sentences. I would visit other church websites and look and study their vision. I needed a vision for First Anna, and I needed it quickly. Then God told me to stop. He told me it would be His vision in His timing. So I stopped and did not worry about it again.

Over a year of pastoring passed before I was given a vision for First Anna. When I received it, I knew it was perfect, not for every church, but for whom our identity is. The vision of First Anna is "Breaking free to pursue Jesus." This vision is geared to both believers and unbelievers. For the churched people the vision is to break free from traditions that have been instilled or the fear of how one is supposed to worship or the condemnation that we live in even though we are forgiven. Christ has unlocked and broken the chains that keep us in our past and living fearful.

Believers can break free and live in freedom. For the unchurched people, we desire for them to break free from the grip of sin and walk in the freedom that is found in Christ alone because He is all that matters.

If God desires transitions, should His desire not be our vision? Does the church you serve reflect the heart of God in 2 Peter 3:9 so that no one may perish? Or does it have the mentality of "us four and no more?" The vision sets the tone for the worship services and the ministries First Anna offers. Regardless of where a person is in their spiritual walk, they leave each service with an understanding of the love Jesus has for us, how to be saved, and how to walk in freedom.

We believe this is the heart of Jesus, and as we follow His heart. It's the passion that keeps us transitioning.

Chapter 7

The Battle

For we are not fighting against flesh-and-blood enemies, but against evil rulers and authorities of the unseen world, against mighty powers in this dark world, and against evil spirits in the heavenly places.
Ephesians 6:12

We are human, but we don't wage war as humans do. We use God's mighty weapons, not worldly weapons, to knock down the strongholds of human reasoning and to destroy false arguments. We destroy every proud obstacle that keeps people from knowing God. We capture their rebellious thoughts and teach them to obey Christ.
2 Corinthians 10:3-5

As this book comes to a close, hopefully you have been challenged. I hope you use this work to help you evaluate the ministry of your church, but also your personal life. I certainly do not have all the answers. Nor is my church the perfect congregation. But I do believe every congregation needs to work through this process of continuing to transition. We're just one story of a church transitioning. There are many. But there needs to be many more.

It is easy as the pastor, staff member, or ministry leader to become frustrated and upset with the churched people. Throughout this book, you probably noticed me sharing some of my frustrations. While my heart and the heart of the staff is that those that are churched would get on board with what God is doing, we realize not everyone is going to get on board. That is difficult for us. And we get frustrated at times.

Allow me to offer a warning: The ultimate problem is not the churched. They can be used as barriers, malcontents, and power brokers to disrupt the church transition. But they are not the true problem. Our battle is a spiritual one. The people problems are simply a symptom of a greater spiritual battle.

The book started with the Holy Spirit because without Him the church cannot transition from the churched to the unchurched. I end this work with a chapter about spiritual warfare because often our frustrations are misplaced and transferred from the spiritual to the physical world.

As you begin the transition of the church you serve, a key verse to remember is found in 2 Corinthians 4:4: "Satan, who is the god of this world, has blinded the minds of those who don't believe. They are unable to see the glorious light of the Good News." Many of the leadership battles you face in the physical realm are derivatives of the battle in the spiritual, unseen world.

You will ask yourself and others in leadership, "How are they not getting this? Look at the lives being changed?" No matter the good that happens or salvations or people finding freedom, this verse is key. For some, unfortunately, their minds have been blinded.

Understand me clearly. In no way am I questioning the salvations of the churched. They are people that sincerely love God but have "grown up" in the church and have certain expectations. When something different from what they expect occurs, resistance is met, and they take defensive positions because their minds have been blinded. Tragically, many are content with their salvation and prefer the comfort of days ago, living and remembering the past and neglecting the present and future.

At one of our business meetings, a man approached one of our elders and was in the process of telling him how bad the church was. He mentioned how I needed to put things back in place the way once were. He desired that I go somewhere else and ruin another church. The elder stopped him and asked a question, "Are your complaints Scriptural or just preferences?" The man responded, "Preferences, but you don't understand." The elder then said that he appreciated his concerns but unless there were Scriptural issues with how First Anna was going, then the complaint was not valid. I am blessed with good elders.

A few months later, this same elder called me and was talking about spiritual warfare. Since the interaction with that church member after the business meeting, his eyes were opened to everything that was happening in the unseen. Spiritual battles can cause people to take offense to all kinds of issues, many of which are imagined. But rather than allowing the Holy Spirit to renew their minds, they continue to walk in blindness to who the real enemy is. They neglect how the real enemy does not want to see First Anna continue down the path of transitioning.

Since many of our people are new to church, they hear on a regular basis a brief synopsis of spiritual warfare. I want them to know it's real. I want them to know how to combat the enemy.

Churched people often have good intentions. Many of them cling to traditions and how church was when they were growing up because in that, they discovered comfort and salvation. Many have the mindset that if it worked for them, then it can work for others. It's an understandable attitude, but it's also immature. While the intentions are good, the enemy twists these intentions and makes them believe that if a church does not "do church" the way it used to or the way they prefer, then either it is not really a church, or they do not need to be a part of it.

The good intentions that the churched people hold on to, the enemy takes and twists. Even though as believers we have the chains unlocked. We are free in Christ.

The churches that resist transitioning are in bondage because they buy into the lie of the enemy that church is about them and their preferences. The enemy wants to keep them from worshipping our Savior. The enemy wants to keep those who are trapped in place, and he will use the lure of sin to cage people. By resisting freedom in Jesus, churches and churched people become enslaved to religion. That's exactly where the enemy wants them, completely blinded and completely ineffective.

Our enemy is extremely smart and cunning and knows how to best attack us. After all, he has had thousands of years to perfect his craft. The Holy Spirit was sent to give us the power to be more than conquerors, to walk in victory. We win because Jesus wins. And every church that begins to transition will see the power lead to fruit. So don't exist as a defeated church.

Transition and become a church with a heart for the lost.

Afterword

"The master said, 'Well done, my good and faithful servant. You have been faithful in handling this small amount, so now I will give you many more responsibilities. Let's celebrate together!'"
Matthew 25:23

Here is my prayer. Regardless of how long I serve at First Anna. Regardless of how old I get. I pray that we will continue to transition. There are various things I would change at First Anna due to me preferring another way, but to do so would mean I am setting up the church the way *I* want it, the way *I* prefer it. To do so would mean that I am more concerned with having church services and making decisions that make me happy.

Nothing at First Anna is about me. Our desire as a staff and church is not to make First Anna look good, but rather we exist to make God look good. We will do what it takes for that to occur. Salvations and discipleship are keys for us. As we continue to transition, we are believing and expecting even more.

If you are a pastor reading this book, then you probably understand much, if not all, of what I am trying to convey. There are hard decisions that are made on a regular basis. Sometimes, as we are weighing what to do, our minds wander and thoughts enter our head, "What am I doing here?" "Am I equipped to be doing this?" Hang in there. You are equipped, and you are the right person for the job.

If you are a staff member or church leader, understand the role your pastor serves. He does not have all the answers, but many people expect him to have these answers. He has concerns he is carrying with him that you will never know about because he is protecting you and others in the church. You may not agree with the decisions that are made, but it is his role to make these decisions. What the pastor needs from you is support and understanding. I once thought naively, "Man, pastors have it easy. They preach and go out to eat." I wish that was even a small amount of my job. I am open and honest with the staff at First Anna, probably more than I should be.

There are a few items I do not share, but most are because we are in this together. And I want them to understand where I am coming from in regards to First Anna.

Transitioning. The mission of Jesus. That is the desire of First Anna: To seek the lost and point them to the One that can save them. For all the headaches that accompany following the mission of Jesus, there is no greater joy than seeing people when they grasp salvation, healing, and freedom. After all, those three words describe Jesus, and

First Anna wants to be known as a place where people of all kinds of backgrounds and mistakes and successes can come as one and worship and be a church in transition.

28108384R00045

Made in the USA
Lexington, KY
05 December 2013